SEVEN DAYS IN THE VALLE

BAJA CALIFORNIA'S WINE COUNTRY CUISINE

7 DAYS IN THE VALLE

By: W. Scott Koenig

www.AGringoInMexico.com

Scott@AGringoInMexico.com

San Diego, California USA

Editor: Nicholas Gilman

www.GoodFoodMexico.com

Mexico City, Mexico

SOCIAL MEDIA

Instagram: @agringoinmexico

Facebook: agringoinmexico

Twitter: wskoenig

YouTube: WScottKoenig

Cover Photo: Corazon de Tierra
Overleaf Photo: L.A. Cetto

eBook ISBN: 978-1-7321020-0-2

Trade Paperback ISBN: 978-1-7321020-1-9

San Diego, California USA

DEDICATION

To Mom, who threatened to haunt me from the grave if I didn't.

Christine Koenig, 1942-2017

FOREWORD

When I first came to live in Mexico, over 25 years ago, I had a vague idea of what the west coast of the country encompassed. Other than a brief visit to the hippy enclave of Puerto Escondido, I managed to stay away. It was common knowledge that Tijuana and Acapulco were best avoided so I concentrated my travels on the interior.

It was not until well past the turn of the millennium that I managed to trudge across the dreary border at San Ysidro and board a bus to Ensenada, capital of the fish taco. By then I was well ensconced in the culinary world and my ignorance of this glorious foodie mecca had become an embarrassing gap in my gastronomic experience. My eyes were opened.

Let's make one thing clear: the Valle de Guadalupe that spreads east of Ensenada center is no Loire Valley. Nor is it the "Mexican Napa" as some creative Department of Tourism types would have it known. This, the country's largest wine producing region, is very much its own thing. It is not spectacularly beautiful nor is it fussy/precious. There's nothing colonial nor Aztec. But it's still Mexico, with all its loveable, funky imperfection. Ramshackle casas topped by corrugated tin roofs sit unashamedly in front of orderly vineyards bursting with ripening grapes. Rolling hills are not all that verdant. But there is beauty; one only has to focus on the details. Refined yet rustic and relaxed restaurants headed by some of the best chefs I know, offer unpretentious dishes based on the area's exquisite *material prima* from sea and land. Superb tempranillo and chardonnay wines are sampled at breathtaking wineries designed by cutting edge architecture firms. And people welcome with open arms.

When I finally got to know the "Valle" it quickly became my favorite gustatory retreat in the country. I'll be back, and soon…

Nicholas Gilman, Good Food Mexico
Mexico City, Mexico

Nicholas Gilman is a food writer and restaurant critic based in Mexico City; he is author of Good Food in Mexico City: Food Stalls, Fondas and Fine Dining, a contributor to The Guardian, Food and Travel, Food & Wine, The New York Times and others. His website is www.goodfoodmexico.com

ACKNOWLEDGEMENTS

I conceived this book in 2017 while assisting the Culinary Institute of America's media department in the preparation of their 2018 documentary about Baja California. The filming took place over seven days, hence the title. Thanks to CIA Media Director John Barkley and his talented and hard-working crew for including me in their adventure in telling the story of Mexico's most recent culinary movement.

I met Ruth Alegria in Acapulco in 2013 during the first World Forum on Mexican Gastronomy. She has since become a friend and mentor and has introduced me to the wider Mexican culinary world. Ruth also served a crucial role during the development and filming of this and other CIA films on Mexican cuisine.

Since this is my first book, I want to thank some who were there for me when I started writing as 'el Gringo.' To Fernando Gaxiola and Martin San Román for introducing me to Baja California wine and cuisine; to Carla White and Ramón Toledo for providing my first online publishing opportunities; and to los bros Plascencia – Javier, Juan José (Tana) and Julian – for their hospitality and generosity of time during several key early interviews.

Thanks to Jeffrey Merrihue and Nicholas Gilman for inviting me to write for FoodieHub (now XTremeFoodies.tv) and for supporting the 2015 nomination of La Cocina de Doña Esthela as "World's Best Breakfast." Further thanks to Nick for his friendship and editing skills on this book. I've become a better writer and a more discerning diner due to his always on point, usually hilarious instruction.

My friend chef Flor Franco once said, "The Valle is very protective of its own. You are either welcome as part of the community, or you're not." I'm very thankful to all the Valle de Guadalupe chefs, winemakers, restaurateurs, hoteliers, tour guides and others who have welcomed my family, friends and I as part of your community. This book is for you.

INTRODUCTION

When I began writing about food and culture in the Guadalupe Valley (better known by its Spanish name, the *Valle de Guadalupe*) in 2012, the murmur of "Baja Med" – coastal European, Asian and Mexican influenced cooking crafted with ingredients from Baja California – had just begun to seduce curious palates across the border in Southern California. Soon, the international travel and culinary press would discover Baja California's wine country and the rest of Mexico would begin to take notice of and herald the arrival of the country's "newest cuisine".

The chef-driven food movement in Baja California began in 2002 when Sonoran Jair Tellez opened Laja in the Valle de Guadalupe (near Ensenada, 90 minutes from the US-Mexico border). The much-lauded restaurant still serves elegant dishes fashioned from local ingredients — including produce and herbs from the restaurant's onsite garden, livestock from nearby ranches and seafood from the Pacific and the Sea of Cortez. Laja was the Valle's first fine dining restaurant and a huge hit with Mexico's growing middle class. Based on its success, similar concepts began to take root and sprout.

The Valle breeds and imports chefs eager to help define Baja California cuisine — and simultaneously enjoy the freedom of experimentation its very lack of definition allows. "Baja California is one of the youngest states of the Mexican republic," chef Diego Hernandez of Corazon de Tierra explains. "Here, we are not bound by centuries of tradition like in Puebla, Oaxaca or the Yucatán. In the Valle, we are free to experiment."

At the opposite end of the culinary spectrum, Esthela Martínez of La Cocina de Doña Esthela has demonstrated that Mexico's traditional cuisine – in her case the rustic country cooking of Sinaloa – can exist side-by-side with more experiential proposals such as the Modern Mexican dishes served at Corazon de Tierra and Malva. Her breakfast-only cocina, located at the end of a dirt road, has become a mecca for aficionados of home-style northern Mexican cooking. Explaining her recipe for success in this region better known for fine dining options, Esthela confides, "Everything I cook is made with love and passion."

What unites all seven chefs included in this book is dedication to experimentation, passion for local food and wine, symbiosis with their neighbors and a deep, soulful connection with the bucolic countryside.

Their stories share common themes but are as varied as their backgrounds. Featured are a chef from America's deep south who earned his Michelin star in Germany, a Tijuana-based cook of Spanish Mediterranean descent who hunts the backcountry for his meat and game, and a native son of Ensenada whose restaurant ranks among San Pellegrino's Latin America's 50 Best.

During interviews conducted for this book, these and several others reflect on the Valle's past, present and uncertain future. This hard-scrabble region struggles with drought and fire, which burns close to its precarious position of becoming an international tourist destination. A percentage of the proceeds will benefit the all-volunteer El Porvenir Fire Department.

W. Scott Koenig, A Gringo in Mexico
San Diego, California, USA

TABLE OF CONTENTS

DAY 1

"EVERY DAY, YOU VOTE WITH YOUR FORK."

Drew Deckman
Deckman's en El Mogor

The Mogor Badan vineyard in the Valle de Guadalupe drapes across a landscape of gently rolling hills, live oaks, grapevines and ranch houses; it tempts with wine-tinted, sun-dappled respite. The vineyard is home to one of Baja California's most popular restaurants, Deckman's en El Mogor. Its namesake Drew Deckman is the region's most vociferous proponent for the use of only "...the freshest, most hyper-local and zero-kilometer ingredients."

At Deckman's, even the dining room is made of sustainable materials — walls are built with a series of stacked hay bales covered in adobe and topped with a roof of recycled corrugate tin. "Drew is known for promoting sustainability and cooking with fire," says fellow chef Roberto Alcocer. During service, Deckman can usually be found goggle-clad and head-down in his outdoor kitchen, surrounded by the smoke from an ever-expanding bank of adjustable, coal-black Santa Maria grills.

At his handmade brick hearth, the chef flips thick 900-gram rib-eyes of grain-fed cattle sourced from a small ranch in Mexicali. He lightly sears abalone from an aquaculture farm just south of Ensenada. He grills orchard-fresh vegetables from the vineyard's garden — just enough to accentuate their full flavor. It's all done over oak or carob wood that he collects from a grove on Mogor Badan's property.

"I'M NOT REALLY A NEW AGE SORT OF PERSON,
BUT WHEN I CAME TO THE VALLE DE GUADALUPE
FOR THE FIRST TIME, I FELT LIKE I'D BEEN HERE
BEFORE. IT MADE MY SOUL FEEL CALM."

DREW DECKMAN

On the success of his restaurant and cuisine, the chef – a former philosophy major – reflects; "There are all these other places opening (in the valley), but our number of visitors keeps going up. People get our message and want to enjoy and understand the ranch experience we're sharing. They care about what they're eating."

After earning his Michelin star in Germany and working in various kitchens in Europe, Deckman decided to settle down, cook and raise a family in the Valle de Guadalupe. He explains that "There's a band around the earth where wine can be produced, and I think the culinary IQ and the quality of people is higher in these regions. I happen to be neighbors with some of the coolest and most intelligent people I've ever met in all of my travels. If you need to ask why I'm here, just look around. This is pretty incredible."

DAY 2

"EVERYTHING IS MADE WITH LOVE & PASSION."

Esthela Martínez
La Cocina de Doña Esthela

Love is the common ingredient stirred into all the sumptuous Sinaloa-style dishes that Doña Esthela Martínez creates, be it in her restaurant's traditional clay oven, over her kitchen stove or in the deep covered pit outside, where she slowly roasts her famous *borrego tatemado* (charred lamb). "Everything I cook, I make with love and passion," Esthela explains. A bit of her soul informs every dish she serves to a typically full house of expectant and adoring diners.

During Baja California's high season, there can be a wait of up to an hour or more to procure a table at La Cocina de Doña Esthela. It's only accessible via one of the many dirt roads that run through the center of the Valle. But the lines are well worth the payoff of Esthela's plates of hearty breakfast fare.

Esthela is a home cook of humble origins. She and her family opened the restaurant in 2010, initially as a small store next her home. She began by selling burritos, tacos and tamales to hungry farm workers. "First one came, then two. Then eventually they told their friends and we were busy all the time," Esthela recalls.

"MY HOME HERE IN THE VALLE DE GUADALUPE IS ALSO YOUR HOME. I DO WHAT I DO WITH LOVE AND PASSION AND I DO IT EVERY DAY."

ESTHELA MARTÍNEZ

The cast and crew of a telenovela filming across the road at winery Lomita in 2012 officially "discovered" Esthela and gathered in her dining room every morning for a hearty breakfast before they started their workday. In 2015, her *machaca con huevos* (dried and shredded beef with eggs) was awarded "Best Breakfast in the World" by FoodieHub (nominated by the author) and she has subsequently expanded the restaurant to include more dining space and tables to accommodate the growing crowds who gather outside.

Must-try dishes are Esthela's *gorditas* (stuffed corn cakes) with *chorizo*, *borrego* and other fillings, *chicharron en salsa verde* (fried pork skin in *tomatillo* sauce), *elote* (fresh corn) pancakes, *birria de borrego* (a spiced stew of lamb) and of course, her award-winning *machaca*. Warm, just-made corn and flour tortillas, beans and a mild, slightly salty farmer's cheese are served with every breakfast. Esthela's marmalade-filled *empanadas* are great *para llevar* (to-go) for sweet snacking later.

DAY 3

"WE ONLY DO 'VALLE FOOD' HERE."

Roberto Alcocer
Malva

According to chef Roberto Alcocer of Malva, the elements that define cooking in the Valle de Guadalupe are, "the use of fire, wood and charcoal. Respecting the ingredients, and not doing too much to them. Ingredients need to be fresh. If you don't have your own orchard here, there is one nearby where you can buy the best. You serve only the highest quality seafood, of course."

Alcocer moved to Ensenada from Chiapas with his family at age seven. As a culinary student and young chef, he traveled to France, England and around Mexico to learn and work in a number of renowned restaurants, including Enrique Olvera's Pujol, widely considered "ground zero" of Modern Mexican cuisine. He returned to Ensenada and inaugurated Malva in 2014.

The restaurant's dining room and kitchen enjoy the shade of a large thatched roof *palapa*. Its situation on a hill above the Mina Penelope winery affords an expansive view of the nearby Santo Tomas vineyards, a stand of Italian cypress and the gentle ebb and flow of grapevine-etched hills typical of the Valle's landscape.

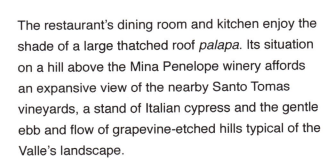

At Malva, Alcocer prepares a rustic country version of Modern Mexican cuisine. Vegetables are gathered from an onsite garden. Sheep and goats are raised in expansive pens on a rise just above the vineyard. "We feed and treat them as we want; and we sacrifice them ourselves," the chef explains.

"THIS IS A PLACE OF SEASONS. I ONCE WROTE AN ARTICLE CALLED 'VALLE DE GUADALUPE: WHORE OF THE SUMMER' BECAUSE A LOT OF PEOPLE WOULD OPEN UP A TEMPORARY RESTAURANT FOR THREE MONTHS AND THEN LEAVE WHEN FALL CAME. NOW THE VALLE IS MORE POPULAR YEAR-ROUND."

ROBERTO ALCOCER

The chef recently began a collaboration with winemaker Veronica Santiago at Mina Penelope to produce his own wines which are designed to pair with Malva's seasonal tasting menus and á la carte dishes. The first vintage includes a hearty malbec, a dry and refreshing malbec-based rosado and a grenache that tastes of red fruit and a bit of spice.

"This restaurant has been the chicken that lays the golden eggs," Alcocer boasts. "I don't think that's right, but in Mexico, we don't have geese." Not one to rest on laurels – such as having Malva consistently listed one of San Pellegrino's Top 120 Mexican Restaurants – the chef limits his time pursuing other projects to ensure the flavors at Malva reflect his exacting standards. "There is Baja cuisine, there is Valle cuisine and there is Roberto cuisine," he emphasizes.

DAY 4

"IN BAJA, WE ARE FREE TO EXPERIMENT."

Miguel Angel Guerrero
La Esperanza

Miguel Angel Guerrero, chef at La Esperanza, stopped practicing law in the 90's and began experimenting with dishes that combined Mexican recipes with Mediterranean and Asian traditions. The result – which he copyrighted as "Baja Med" – jumpstarted the careers of some of Baja California's most notable chefs. Baja Med became a regional catchphrase and quickly caught on nationally, then internationally as the byword used to describe Mexico's "newest cuisine".

A Hallmark of Baja California cuisine is its ability to surprise. The chef elaborates: "In Baja California, we are free to experiment and make new dishes. You couldn't do that in Puebla or Oaxaca. Those Mexican states have over five hundred years of culinary history. They don't want you to mess it up."

Guerrero's Baja Med cooking blends the traditions of three global culinary regions. First is the diversity of the cuisine in Mexico itself. Guerrero says, "Much of our food comes from the kitchens of the Yucatán, Michoacán, Guerrero and Oaxaca. From them, we inherit our chilies, tortillas and salsas." He lists Asia as Baja Med's second influence, as the Chinese and Japanese brought their sauces, sushi and kitchen techniques to the region.

"A LOT OF PEOPLE SAY THAT VALLE IS THE NEXT NAPA VALLEY, BUT IT'S NOT. WE DON'T WANT IT TO BE NAPA VALLEY, LIKE DISNEYLAND. WE DON'T WANT MICKEY MOUSE HERE."

MIGUEL ANGEL GUERRERO

The third and final element – the "Med" in Baja Med – Guerrero credits to his familial roots. "My people come from the Mediterranean part of Spain, which has a similar climate to Baja California. Like near the Mediterranean, here we have vineyards, olive oil, similar vegetables and herbs."

When the chef isn't at La Esperanza, located in the verdant and well-tended vineyards of L.A. Cetto, or one of his Tijuana restaurants, he's somewhere with a small band of friends and adventurers who fish and hunt their way up and down the Baja peninsula. Guerrero literally captures the essence of Baja California's bounty – guts and cleans it – and puts it on the menu.

It's not unusual to find something at La Esperanza that the chef buckshot or spearfished himself. A savory burrito of bow-hunted venison. Grouper and halibut collars in *adobado* (a vinegar-based sauce with chilies and other spices). Seared jackrabbit loin served with medallions of tuna. "My family always took me diving and fishing. Those experiences help build character," the chef explains.

DAY 5

"LEAVE ME ALONE. I'M MAKING TORTILLAS."

Sheyla Alvarado
Traslomita

Traslomita – the seasonal, campestre-style restaurant located on the grounds of Lomita winery – is accessed by exiting the tasting room's large wooden doors, then walking down a gentle dirt path lined with rows of Merlot grapevines. The spacious dining area and rustic kitchen are situated in and around a number of shade trees and partly covered with overhead awnings of stretched fabric. In this idyllic garden setting, young chef Sheyla Alvarado continues the locavore tradition established by her neighbors and mentors.

"I'm lucky because I get to hang out with great chefs like Javier Plascencia, Miguel Angel Guerrero and Roberto Alcocer," she muses. "I remember coming to Valle as a child with my parents: there was nothing, only a couple of restaurants. It's the chefs working here who put it on the map. The people who live here have welcomed us outsiders and are really good to us. And the land provides us with animals, vegetables and wine, which is awesome."

She enjoys the peace and isolation that her pastoral setting provides: "Sometimes, I just put on my headphones and say: Leave me alone, I'm making tortillas!" Sheyla landed at Traslomita based on a recommendation from the restaurant's founder and former executive chef Humberto Avila. The restaurant was a good fit as she learned to cook with wood ovens at La Contra in Ensenada, then refined her style and presentation working alongside Ryan Steyn at El Cielo Winery in the Valle.

"WORKING IN VALLE PROVIDES A DIFFERENT KIND OF LIFE. WE DON'T HAVE CLOSED KITCHENS — WE GET TO SEE THE SUNSET EVERY EVENING. I GET TO SEE THE PEOPLE HERE EATING OUT IN NATURE, WHICH CREATES A BOND FOR ME TO THIS PLACE. IT MAKES ME REALLY APPRECIATE THE ENVIRONMENT AND WANT TO MAKE IT BETTER WHILE BEING RESPONSIBLE."

SHEYLA ALVARADO

The long tables at Traslomita are conducive to the "family style" dishes served here. "What we do is try to remind people of when they used to hang out at Grandma's kitchen and families would get together to share food." Her signature dishes include tender roasted chicken, an excellent *ceviche*-like *aguachile negro* of shrimp and succulent, shredded *borrego* (mutton), served with warm, house-made corn tortillas.

Alvarado was born in the neighboring Mexican state of Sonora but moved to Baja California when she turned eighteen to study culinary arts in Ensenada. "I still use ingredients from Sonora, but my love of Baja California cuisine has changed my influences," she confides.

DAY 6

"THE GROUND CONTAINS THE FLAVOR OF THE REGION."

Diego Hernandez
Corazon de Tierra

Corazon de Tierra, located on the grounds of acclaimed winery Vena Cava, has been lauded as one of San Pellegrino's 50 Best Restaurants in Latin America. The man behind its success, Diego Hernandez, bears none of the countenance of a celebrity chef. Peering out from behind his trademark round spectacles, Hernandez is one of the Valle's most avid proponents of local sourcing. "Here in the restaurant, I put a lot of pressure on the process of how we grow our vegetables, as well as on all the animals and seafood that we serve," he insists.

The chef named his restaurant Corazon de Tierra – heart of the earth – to acknowledge the importance that regional terroir plays in his food. "The Valle's soil contains the flavors of the region," he explains. "It doesn't make sense to me to use local food if you grow things in the greenhouse. Or to feed animals food that doesn't taste like it's from this land. The produce must be grown in the pH of our soil and then fed to our animals, so they possess a similar balance. The seafood should taste of the brininess of our ocean."

Hernandez elaborates: "The flavors we get in Ensenada, Tijuana or Mexicali are from the same region, but very different. But there are always constants — corn, tortillas, chilies and a lot of seafood. And we use some Asian touches. That blend is what makes Baja California style cooking so unique."

"WHAT IS THE 'FLAVOR' OF THE VALLE DE GUADALUPE?
TO ME, EVERYTHING TASTES OF SALT AND OLIVE OIL."

DIEGO HERNANDEZ

"Baja California is one of the youngest territories of the Mexican republic, named a state in 1960," he continues. "Our community is made of people from all over the country. That's why our culture is so rich, and the cuisine is so diverse. When we have people from Oaxaca working here, for example, we learn more about moles. Our food has definite roots in Mexican food and culture. Our menu can change just based on who is in the kitchen."

Reflecting on life and work in the Valle, Hernandez concludes, "The Valle is a very interesting place. People usually only visit here three days a week, so we end up with spare time on our hands." It's then that the chef can continue to experiment with his fascinating blend of fresh ingredients with international influences.

"IT'S RARE TO HAVE A BAD MEAL IN THE VALLE."

Javier Plascencia
Finca Altozano

Javier Plascencia's Finca Altozano is one of the most successful restaurants in the Valle de Guadalupe. Starting in the early 1960's, his family founded many of Tijuana's most popular eateries – Casa Plasencia *(sic)*, Villa Sevarios, Caesar's and a growing chain of Giuseppe's pizzerias – and their culinary talent and business acumen inform the chef in every restaurant he helps open.

Plascencia chose the Valle de Guadalupe as the site for Finca Altozano due to its proximity to fresh farm ingredients as well as the location's nearly mythical allure. "This valley has a very special vibe to it," he says; "It's like old world. Like arriving at Finca: you drive down dirt roads and end up at a special place in the middle of nowhere. The people here are friendly, the wines just keep getting better and better and so do the restaurants and the food. It's rare that you have a bad meal in the Valle."

The hearty platters of country fare he and his staff serve at the campestre-style Finca Altozano are the antithesis of the delicate, meticulously-plated dishes of Modern Mexican cuisine he sends out at Mision 19, the game-changing Tijuana eatery he opened in 2011.

"MY GOAL IS TO EVENTUALLY RETIRE IN THE VALLE DE GUADALUPE, BUILD A FAMILY RANCH AND DRINK RED WINE UNDER AN OLD OAK TREE."

JAVIER PLASCENCIA

Some of the highlights on Finca Altozano's menu are the grilled quail, Mediterranean style octopus, *caja China* cooked lamb and country salads that chef de cuisine Pedro Peñuelas tosses from produce he's gathered from the restaurant's garden. There are also pens of sheep and goats for birria and other dishes. Plascencia leases the restaurant's land from the Magoni winemaker family whose vines surround the restaurant perimeter.

Reflecting on the international attention the Valle de Guadalupe has received, chef Plascencia says, "There's a lot of media about the Valle. It's happening now, and we're going to get more and more people. We need to be careful not to get too commercial. Of course, we want guests at the restaurants and the wineries want to sell wine, but without affecting the charm of this place."

ABOUT THE AUTHOR

San Diego-based lifestyle writer W. Scott Koenig has traveled throughout Mexico and Baja California for over twenty years. He founded AGringoInMexico.com in 2012 to report on Mexican travel destinations, food, culture and adventure. He is considered a major social media influencer in San Diego and Baja California.

Scott also writes columns for DiningOut San Diego, SanDiegoRed.com and DiscoverBaja.com. He has been published at NewWorlder, Baja.com, The Baja Times, Destino Los Cabos Magazine, The Oaxaca Times and The San Diego Free Press.

He is the Food Expert for Baja California for XtremeFoodies.tv, (formerly FoodieHub), an international culinary site curated by over 275 global experts.

Scott organizes and conducts culinary tours of Baja California and has helped fix film and video productions in the region for the Cooking Channel, the BBC, Public Television and the Culinary Institute of America.

He is also the owner of Koenig Creative LLC in San Diego and has counted several Fortune 1000 companies as clients. He has over 30 years of experience in marketing, creative direction and graphic design.

A PERCENTAGE OF THE PROCEEDS FROM
THIS BOOK BENEFIT THE EL PORVENIR
VOLUNTEER FIRE DEPARTMENT

CONTRIBUTE TO A GRINGO IN MEXICO
AT PATREON.COM/AGRINGOINMEXICO

Your patronage in the form of a donation or ongoing sponsorship helps fund our efforts to discover, experience and report on Mexican food, culture and events. Patrons are eligible for: invitations to special tours, meals and events; early and exclusive content; and other benefits and promotions as they become available.

CPSIA information can be obtained at www.ICGtesting.com
Printed in the USA
BVIW12n0016290418
514721BV00006B/181